365 DAYS

OF INSPIRATIONAL

QUOTES HONORING MEN

There Is A King In You

VALENCIA ESTHER QUEEN

Published And Distributed By
Valencia Esther Queen Publication
Long Beach, California
(562) 423-6877
Email:valenciaequeen@yahoo.com

Packaging/Consulting
Professional Publishing House
1425 W. Manchester Ave. Ste B
Los Angeles, California 90047
323-750-3592
Email: professionalpublishinghouse@yahoo.com
www.Professionalpublishinghouse.com

Cover and Interior design: TWASolutions.com
First printing March 2015
ISBN: 978-0-9861945-0-4
10987654321

For inquiries contact: valenciaequeen@yahoo.com

Dedication

This book is dedicated to every man that is in pursuit of the king within.

January

January 1

Men, 75% of you will find it hard to believe how great you are. The other 25% will show how great you are.

January 2

Strength is not only required to lift heavy objects, it is also an attribute that is needed in your mind, body, and soul.

January 3

You are an extraordinary gift from God! Acknowledge your brother and watch the gifts continue to unfold.

January 4

Be who you are! Expect nothing in return.
You are one of a kind.

January 5

You can search a life time for answers you
already have within.

January 6

Be patient for the wind. Your time will come
to soar; just like an eagle it will be effortlessly.

January 7

Material things bring temporary
gratification into your life.

January 8

Be love and not expect it in return, but
embrace it when it's returned.

January 9

Words can have a negative impact in your life.
Use words that will uplift you and
the people around you.
(PUT AN END TO DISRESPECT!)

January 10

You are a gift to the world, we need you! The gift you carry is not battery-operated, it only need's a heart.

January 11

Here is one way to fight a battle and win. Simply say, "I love you."

January 12

What makes you smile?

January 13

Have faith in what you do and have faith in who you can become. Faith is the substance you have within and the evidence is when you manifest it. I aspire you to make it happen.

January 14

Accomplishing goals get you closer to your purpose. Create goals for purpose.

January 15

Love never change we do.

January 16

Everybody born into this world is born to love
and desire to be loved.

January 17

Forgive yourself even if others don't.

January 18

Mere words can't describe how much we need
you that's why we shout, we scream and cry
because we need you.

January 19

Men, material item are not above you. The
importance of a man is not defined by the have
and the have not's.

January 20

Men, grow beyond personalities. Jesus was the
only one born perfect.

January 21

Men, there is no me/us/we without you.

January 22
Inspiring "Men" Because, You're worth it!

January 23
Men, who am I, who are they, who are we not to honor and respect you.

January 24
Men, as you learn more about yourself don't hate the dirt you see! Dig deeper and find that hidden diamond.

January 25
Men, you're priceless!

January 26
Men, life is like driving a stick shift car. If you don't switch gears you'll burn out.

January 27
Men, the only thing you should take personal is the death of Jesus Christ, because He died for you.

January 28

Men, I have faith and confidence in you!

January 29

Men, life has a way of slowing you down, so that you can enjoy the moments it has to offer.

January 30

Men, Love is the greatest emotion given to mankind! Once love is filtered out, man can only experience Anger, Sadness and Fear.

January 31

People only have the power you give them. If you don't know your enemy, you could be the next Samson!

February

February 1

Discover who you are, so that the glory of the
Lord can shine among us through you.

February 2

Men, rejoice and express intense enjoyment.

February 3

Nothing can stand against the Great I AM. He
is not moved by circumstances. He is moved
when you call Him!

February 4

Don't live or fulfill other's prophecy!
Write your own story.

February 5

True happiness comes from within you, yes you!
The power to create Love, Joy and Happiness
dwell only in you.

February 6

The best in you is waiting to shine in a world
that is lacking brightness.

February 7

A perfect man walked the earth to show you
what He had to go through in order to conquer
and win!

February 8

I inspire you not to quit and never give up!

February 9

If you focus on who you are not, then you will never be! Focus on who you are then you will become the great I AM.

February 10

Use obstacles as steps and situations as a rail to keep your balance!

February 11

Knowledge IS power, but Prayer is POWERFUL! Combine the 2.

February 12

Money is not evil nor is it the
root of happiness.

February 13

There is no better time than NOW! Remember
time is like sand it will slip through your fingers.

February 14

If you were cubit would you make people love
or would you love people?

February 15

Peace is free, but when you give it away
there is a price to pay.

February 16

You were born in your birthday suit! No matter what comes or what goes don't try to dress yourself with it.

February 17

A negative mindset can dig a ditch; a positive mindset can dig trenches to build a building to leave a legacy.

February 18

Stand tall even if you do not feel like you are walking on solid ground.

February 19
Keep the faith TRY again!

February 20
You are great! There is nothing He created greater than you.

February 21
When a bird flies he uses the wind that's against him in order to fly higher i.e. let the trouble launch you higher.

February 22
Sometimes you have to let go to have peace. Peace is priceless and it only comes from God.

February 23

There is always a cloud of witnesses and a host of
people cheering for you! Be encouraged.

February 24

If there is any pain in your heart or mind be
free! I pray that you use it to make
you a wiser person.

February 25

God moves based on your position in Him,
not your performance.

February 26

I realize and recognize that your
heart is over looked.

February 27

Seek the pleasure of your heart and happiness
will fall at your feet.

February 28

Use your past as a mountain to step over your
next valley; wisdom and experience are good
teachers.

March

March 1

You are more powerful than you think feel or imagine. Read the book of Proverbs build yourself up; let no one bring you down.

March 2

Never think you're too far down to get up.

March 3

The truth is in the heart of every Man.

March 4

If they don't walk with you, you must walk alone.

March 5

Never step on a Man's pride.

March 6

God is getting ready to turn things
around; participate and anticipate,
be exceedingly glad!

March 7

Stay focused, stay in the game, go
through and don't stop!

March 8

I give much honor and respect to you all.

March 9

Don't let nothing bring you down,
remember it's NOTHING.

March 10

Look upon a man with honor and you
will see a reflection of God.

March 11

A man is irreplaceable.

March 12

The substance of things hoped for...don't
except to see it just believe.

March 13

If you are in a time zone that appear to be going no where; it is only God re-positioning you.

March 14

I thank you for your protection, your strength and your wisdom. Most importantly your failures and setbacks proves your ability to come back!

March 15

You lead to show the way when we are lost.

March 16

Your life is like a quarterbacked you are the most wanted and the most needed person in life.

March 17

Respect all Men, it just might be Christ.

March 18

No one can measure the love you have for your children.

March 19

Emotional pain shouldn't weaken you until you become paralyzed and then lifeless, but don't stay down too long.

March 20

Get in the lane called faith; it's the
lane you can't see!

March 21

When a boy becomes a man, revealing insights
are being developed; no one can create
this image but God.

March 22

Wake up! The world is in
need of your greatness.

March 23

Make room in your heart for love and make
room to be pleased with life and
all it has to offer.

March 24

Wait patiently on The Lord.

March 25

Think outside the box, take broken things and
make them work.

March 26

Focus on the promise, not the problem.

March 27

One thing I clearly understand, there is
no me without you.

March 28

Men always KNOW who you are in the mist of
struggles, in the mist of hard times and
in the mist of chaos.

March 29

God has truly blessed men with a great mind.

March 30

Men you are a perfect gift from God, you inspire me and that's why I inspire you.

March 31

You are amazing.

April

April 1

Men. are special! Rise with and in God's morning glory. Be proud of who you are and change what you don't like.

April 2

You are and will always be God's all time favorite.

April 3

An older wise MAN is more than a celebration, require more, be more, do more and enjoy the rest of your life.

April 4

You're a wise man, believe in thy self.

April 5

Men, the light in you expels darkness.

April 6

Men, you are the bread of life!

April 7

You are God's valuable treasure.

April 8

We deeply need you!

April 9

Our lives would be like a desert without you.

April 10

_____our lives

are empty without you in it.

April 11

The sweat of your brow, the labor upon
your back and the sacrifices you
make are appreciated.

April 12

I declare love not war!

April 13

Anybody that has the opportunity to meet you
should be grateful.

April 14
It is a pleasure to see your smile.

April 15
Once you discover who you are,
change is inevitable.

April 16
Predictable behavior is low creativity.

April 17
Obtain emotional intelligence for logic, for
understanding and for self-awareness.

April 18
Intentions affect everything else.

April 19
Divine purpose will enable courage.

April 20
I Prayed for you, I am Praying for you and will Pray for you.

April 21
Draw a line of demarcation; begin again.

April 22

Here is my combination: Prayer! Faith! Hope!
And Praise!

April 23

How far do you have to travel to
believe in you?

April 24

Disappointment, sadness, sorrow can last one
second, one minute, one hour and one month.
It's up to you.

April 25

Express gratitude, kindness and love
towards yourself.

April 26

All fathers are special and
deeply appreciated.

April 27

Failure in systems that was designed for a
selected few; is success for thy superior self.

April 28

The past is gone! Only you can
make it your future.

April 29

Break free from mental bondage,
it's self created.

April 30

Joy comes from within you!

May

May 1

Adversity isn't the problem, not doing
anything about is.

May 2

Explore the unmeasurable
qualities of your being.

May 3

Be *Your* first priority.

May 4
Break the mode of habits and find
your success story.

May 5
_____ there is no

one like you, bless you and all that you do!
Live the greatness within you.

May 6
The process is to show you that you can do
anything but fail!

May 7

You are as I Am! The victory has already been won.

May 8

You are the keeper of thy brethren and God is the keeper of thine soul.

May 9

Life is an experience LIVE it!

May 10

Thank you for stepping in and taking charge over what I couldn't control.

May 11

Honoring You is my heart's desire.

May 12

I yield with aspiration of your masculinity.

May 13

Psychological discipline is the
throne in your side.

May 14

I see you rising with the sun at an
appointed time.

May 15

He gave us the best of Himself, through you.

May 16

Lack of awareness causes stumbling blocks.

May 17

We can't make it without you!

May 18

We really need you!

May 19
Have Patients with yourself.

May 20
You don't fail - you just awaken.

May 21
Love never change, but it adds to you.

May 22
You're not alone.

May 23

Go all the way, achieve great things now.

May 24

When you speak the universe is
obedient to your command.

May 25

Men, you owe your past no explanation! Stop
replaying, stop repeating, stop visualizing the
negative images and develop your future.

May 26

Your strength is sustaining.

May 27

Be revived! Be renewed! Be restored!

May 28

As long as we are on this earth I will rain with you, I will sow with you and grow with you.

May 29

Spiritual experiences Does Not make logical sense.

May 30

Guilt is owning responsibility as responsibility
is taking control. Get in the position of power.

May 31

God created the earth a habitat for men to
dwell in and He created a place for
himself to dwell in you.

June

June 1

Love you.
Trust you.
Adore you.

June 2

Forgive.

June 3

You did it!
Nobody else could do it.
Remember life is not a competition.

June 4

Thank you for being on my side
Thank you for loving me
Thank you for raising me
Thank you for kindness.

June 5

There are no worries when you are around.
Your presence make it all better.

June 6

The only bridge worth repairing is LOVE.

June 7

Plug into your infinite wisdom.

June 8
The past is gone!

June 9
Dream Again and Again!

June 10
You are not forgotten.

June 11
You can always count on "Love".

June 12
Call it an audible! Change the play.

June 13

Don't bring the demolition ball unless you
have the material to build.

June 14

Take the necessary steps to confront it, so that
you can stand up!

June 15

If you don't decide someone else
will decide for you.

June 16

In order to be stable you need people you can
count on, no man is an island.

June 17

Be passionate about life!

June 18

Harness irritation to do great things.

June 19

Take authority over your territory.

June 20

God has given you the deed of trust.

June 21

Transfer you energy to get there.

June 22

Whatever happens, happens. Is an
excuse not to do anything.

June 23

Come in the volume of a higher purpose.

June 24

Take a daily dose of medication called
LAUGHTER.

June 25

Believe in something! But why
not believe in yourself.

June 26

Stop wasting time - no, stop wasting energy.

June 27

Discern obstacles that will take you off course.

June 28

Respect Authenticity!

June 29

Knowing how to apply knowledge is the principle of wisdom.

June 30

If you focus on the pain of your past you will miss the point of your purpose.

July

July 1

An immature mind often makes an adult
decision but once you mature you
could fix it.

July 2

When you are awaken to life! You just
can't get enough of it!

July 3

Embrace the revelation and
experience the revolution.

July 4

Simple things to you, is "LOVE"
for someone else.

July 5

A man that dares to strive will reach his goals,
regardless of resistance.

July 6

If you had an opportunity to change your life,
Will you do it?

July 7

The challenge with life is figuring
out who you are.

July 8

Travel the road of destiny,
Your purpose will come into alignment.

July 9
The irony of life is not enjoying it.

July 10
Embrace your mantel.

July 11

Pass the *flaming* torch.

July 12
Leave your legacy.

July 13

Age does not build momentum,
experience does.

July 14

You can physically open a jar, but your words
have enough power to move mountain.

July 15

The more you give out, the more
God will download.

July 16

Endurance! Persistence! Determination!
These will connect you to the stream and
the flow will get better.

July 17

Wake up to the change! Understand it's a process and there is no conclusion.

July 18

I never met such a brave heart full of courage until I met you.

July 19

You are great!
You are wonderful!
You are mighty!

July 20

Accumulation of matter will become mass, the spirit is light.

July 21

You make the difference!

July 22

A Divinely Commissioned man, can
manifest supernatural miracles.

July 23

It takes courage, perseverance and
determination to make great things happen.

July 24

You are marvelous!

July 25

Know the truth, walk in the
truth and be free!

July 26

Stop digging up the past, it's
depleting your energy.

July 27

I am committed to lifting you up!

July 28

I adore you!

July 29
Understanding, is the link between
knowledge and wisdom.

July 30
Walk with confidence!
Do not live a defeated life.

July 31
One who devalue you is not worthy of you!

August

August 1

The smallest change in your life can conquer the biggest giant that comes to torment you.

August 2

Jealousy, back biting and envy.
Translations:
I wish I were you!

August 3

A note to powerful men.
When you sit in the same room with other powerful men. Don't fear who's more powerful.

August 4

Experience is an expensive teach, it cost more than books, seminars, research, long hours of studying and a college education.
Don't forget I told you so.

August 5

A person so quick to use an abusive tongue quickly forget who they are and they don't know who you are.

August 6

Change for an exchange!

August 7

Finding yourself or creating yourself every day offers a new beginning.

August 8

Courage and Confidence becomes silent when you really need them most.

August 9

Value yourself now! Value your time now! Do better today than yesterday, because we need you more today than yesterday!

August 10

Emerge out of drowning deep in sorrow. Tears may fall, but as a log floating and drifting on top of water you can emerge and not drown in sorrow.

August 11

I inspire you to be who you know you
are and all of who you are.

August 12

The company you keep is not always people
your thoughts will become your friend. Guard
your mind from negative thoughts by
having mercy towards everyone.

August 13

Some choices can create failing situations, but
these choices are not who you are.

August 14

The most important gift God gave to the earth was and is mankind.

August 15

God prepared the earth as a gift for man, He declare His creation Awesome! Marvelous! Excellent! Great! Magnificent! Wonderful!

August 16

An open heart, mind, and soul has an advantage to grow in life.

August 17

I'm so happy you are not perfect, it's such a
hard image to maintain.

August 18

Utilize time wisely to silence, "Should've
would've could've" time is now!
Not of the essence.

August 19

You win in preparation! You conquer defeat in
persistence! You untangle failure
with right choices!

August 20

Often, people look for one extraordinary big moment! However they never count the billions of ordinary moments that makes life as great as it is.

August 21

Happiness is like a stream and Joy is the living water flowing through it.

August 22

You are a hero! A knight with armor protecting all that you love from hurt, harm and danger.

August 23

You are a distinguished man, your qualities are like no other! Be brave and have courage!

August 24

What is the definition of you?

August 25

Reflect on your personal agenda and
get back to your goals.

August 26

When you don't learn from mistakes
you can't move forward.

August 27

The real truth about mistakes, they are proof
you are on the road to success.

August 28

An idle mind with no new information will revert back to an infant state of being.

August 29

Don't stop learning, your greatest days are ahead.

August 30

You are extremely gifted and talented.

August 31

There is something about your name, you are somebody great!

September

September 1

This month, I want to deeply express my
gratitude by acknowledging all the things
you do every day!

September 2

Thank you for running to me when everyone
else was no where to be found.

September 3

Thank you for having great courage.

September 4

Thank you! Thank you! Thank you!
For simply being who you are!

September 5

Thank you for your diligent hard work.

September 6

Thank you for caring enough to share your knowledge by educating those around you.

September 7

Thank you for reminding the world that team work matters!

September 8

To every Troop! I salute you all with great honor! Thank you, for protecting us, you are important!

September 9
Thank you for sharing your talent
with the world.

September 10
Thank you for a new beginning!

September 11
Thank you! For having faith, believing,
praying and worshipping God.

September 12
Thank you for giving more of your time and
energy to make it happen.

September 13

Thank you for giving and pouring out
your love when I needed it.

September 14

Thank you for being patient!

September 15

Thank you for being a great leader.

September 16

Thank you for words of wisdom, I can still hear
them when you're not around.

September 17

Thank you for standing in the mist of the storm,
your strength got us through every trial.

September 18

Thank you for understanding!

September 19

Thank you for loving me.

September 20

Thank you for seeing greatness in me.

September 21

Thank you for teaching me the
importance of Forgiving!

September 22

Thank you for looking beyond my
failure and faults.

September 23

Thank you for speaking words of kindness!

September 24

Thank you for being my dear friend.

September 25
Thank you for every act of kindness.

September 26
Thank you for being available when I needed you.

September 27
Thank you for being faithful!

September 28
Thank you for opening up doors.

September 29

Thank you for every hug, every kiss,
and every smile.

September 30

Thank you for being gentle, gracious and great!

October

October 1

I hope you have taken in joy and
feel greatly appreciated.

October 2

Capture every rich experience in your
mind body and soul.

October 3

A vision is not only a blissful moment.

October 4

A dream can change the world and action can
shift a nation into the right direction.

October 5

Secret's lie within obstacle and challenges
because they too have purpose.

October 6

No one can make you happy, they can only
entertain you. Happiness is from within.

October 7

Be the one that loves too much.

October 8

There is no stargazes to happiness.

October 9

A man is the Garden of Eden like a woman is hidden treasure. The curiosity of a man will search for the content, but that takes time.

October 10

Remember how powerful you are! You have shown the world that you can conquer anything. I'm proud of you!

October 11

A strong opinion is full of false energy that overlook facts.

October 12
Be the best *You* every day.

October 13
You're the essential key for tomorrow!
Start living.

October 14
Yesterday is gone! I guarantee you, it
will never return.

October 15

Hatred, anger and strife is a camouflage of fear!

October 16

Every **Good idea** is not a God idea. However good ideas are motivational positive stimulant for the mind.

October 17

Loneliness is a deceitful way depression creeps in the mind, no man is an island you're not alone!

October 18
Passion creates dynamic experiences!

October 19
The essence of an alpha male is his ability to lead with his heart.

October 20
Look at the big picture! Offer yourself more of it.

October 21

Recalibrate! We are waiting.

October 22

Endurance is not about speed. It actually wins the race.

October 23

Internally or externally facing an enraged enemy, requires physical and mental stamina is required.

October 24

The brightest sunshine or the darkest room should not shift your vision! Stay focused.

October 25

You're an insatiable MAN!

October 26

Stamina is driven when pressured.

October 27

The edge is the right moment to change your life!

October 28

Size means nothing when you have the
right tools to hit the target.

October 29

Size doesn't matter because power
comes in volume.

October 30

A leader that is driven by power! Can lose the
measure of love in his heart.

October 31

Love enable! And control disable.

November

November 1

Change come in increments not overnight, stay
focus and find a better you! This season
you are the focal point.

November 2

If you really want to become rich, work
like a machine or build one.

November 3

Greed is a short cut to becoming rich, but it's
the longest loneliest route of living miserable.

November 4

Do something you love to fulfill who you are, love again believe again.

November 5

The goal is not to be embracive, the goal is to embrace.

November 6

Be proud of your journey. Go worldwide!

November 7

Legends rise by putting more into their work to create change. When a legend see a problem they become the solution.

November 8

There are 24 hours in a day, spend time digging trenches to build your dreams.

November 9

Rejection is a good sign, you are closer than what you think.

November 10

Be incredible and good at what you do!
Have a brave heart.

November 11

True success is discovering one's own
ability to think.

November 12

A person that only studies his craft and
his competitors will make an excellent
commentator. You must have the will to DO!

November 13

Energy is money and time is money. It's nothing like investing in yourself.

November 14

Undermining your masculinity will weaken your position in the world.

November 15

Celebrate all of your accomplishments, stay positive.

November 16

Except the fact that you are different! You were born with a different purpose and a different goal. Go and pursue!

November 17

Self –sufficient!

November 18

A dream is just an illusion unless action is applied, be diligent!

November 19

Life never calls for a time out. Let's go!

November 20

Past failed experiences is proof to others that you can't win, ***however*** the future is proof that you are expected to win.

November 21

Dreams are not expensive, mistakes are.

November 22

The secret is analyzing your spending habits to get a better return.

November 23

Successful people experience one thing unsuccessful people don't want to experience, "Failure".

November 24
Treat people better than you treat yourself!

November 25
What you create or invent with your imagination is the story people want to hear about and see.

November 26
Work 24 hours a day 7days a week to design your very own master piece.

November 27

Here's a business mentality "Be fearless".

November 28

Don't just leave the world with a memory of you but leave your legacy. A flaming torch that will burn forever.

November 29

Every second is a new starting point.

November 30

Innovator!

December

December 1

Pursue in truth! Purpose is next.

December 2

Authenticity is refreshing! Rebuild.

December 3

What makes your heart smile! Restore.

December 4

A glimpse of love is seen, when you offer grace! Renew.

December 5
Believing in yourself, should be your
biggest influence.

December 6
Experience is a different type of teacher.

December 7
When a man is ready to apply his hands to
form, to create, and to manifest he is free
from fear of the unknown.

December 8
Love, Forgive, Respect
(Never forget)
Love, Forgive, Respect.

December 9
Everyday life is expecting you to live!

December 10
It's ok to want someone, but it's not ok to put
your responsibility on someone.

December 11

If you have no fear of what you may lose, no one or nothing can control you!

December 12

Growth is inevitable! When you want to grow.

December 13

Create a strategic plan to win!

December 14

Awareness of a road doesn't make you a leader, the boldness to travel the road making it successful for others to follow.

December 15

The spirit of God is whom you have your being. The mind of Christ is where you should plant your thinking. Your body is an embassy in which He has dwelling. Grant Him access because ye are little gods.

December 16

Yes! You are responsible for what you respond to.

December 17

Circumstances, situations, trials and tribulations are composed to cultivate your character so that you can effectively live your true purpose.

December 18

Negativity has no ability to help anyone!

December 19

In order to move ahead you must plan new
strategies, start planning for your future.

December 20

Identify yourself and know thy self at all times.
Connect with the image within.

December 21

Deep lows and extreme highs
are equivalent to a roller-coaster ride MAN
must decipher emotions from logic.

December 22

During your season of transformation, other's vision will be obscured, but don't forsake the transformation to adjust their eyesight.

December 23

Important relationship to have. A shepherd, a mentor, a leader, and a friend.

December 24

Stagnation is lack of decision making.

December 25

You are a victor, because of the victory that has been won!

December 26

Exit the amusement park! Emotions is like a personal roller-coaster ride in your mind. Your mind is still spinning, but your feet are planted on solid ground. Exit this vicious cycle!

December 27

You are greater than that, you just haven't accepted the facts yet.

December 28

Focus on the vision not the provision and finish what you started. When the ark is finished you won't be alone.

December 29

Go get it! Even if you have to go through the
eye of the storm!

December 30

Do you know who you really are? Do you really
know who you were really meant to be? What is
your assignment on earth?

December 31

Let all of God's love and majesty flow to you
and through you.

CPSIA information can be obtained at www.ICGtesting.com
Printed in the USA
BVOW05s1859050415

394814BV00001B/1/P